DATE DUE

Contents

© Aladdin Books Ltd 2010

Designed and produced by
Aladdin Books Ltd
PO Box 53987
London SW15 2SF

First published in 2010
by Franklin Watts
338 Euston Road
London NW1 3BH

Franklin Watts Australia
Level 17/207 Kent Street
Sydney NSW 2000

Franklin Watts is a division of
Hachette Children's Books,
an Hachette UK company.
www.hachette.co.uk

All rights reserved
Printed in Malaysia

Scientific consultant: Rob Bowden

A catalogue record for
this book is available
from the British Library.

Dewey Classification:
333.95'39

ISBN 978 07496 9081 6

What's the Issue?

Biofuels are fuels made from organic matter such as wood, crops and animal dung. They can be burnt to make heat or to generate electricity and could help to provide a solution to the world's energy problems.

Most of our energy comes from fossil fuels: gas, coal and oil. Oil also provides liquid fuel for most of the world's cars, trucks and planes. However, burning fossil fuels releases gases that add to global warming. The challenge is to find a cheap, reliable alternative without adding to our environmental problems. Biofuels are a potentially renewable source of energy, but growing large amounts of crops to create energy could use up land and water needed for growing food.

◑ Wood chips *can be burnt to create electricity.*

◉ Cow dung *has been used as a fuel for thousands of years.*

What Are Biofuels?

Biofuels are renewable fuels made from biomass, which is any material that comes from living or recently dead plants, animals, fungi and bacteria. Rubbish, animal waste, wood chips, energy crops like sugar cane and even seaweed can be used to generate heat and electricity, and to make fuels for cars, trucks and planes.

Biofuels can be solid, such as wood or peat. They can also be liquid, such as the ethanol or diesel produced from crops, or they can be a gas, such as the biogas (methane) produced from animal or human dung.

◖ A Store for Solar Energy

The original source of the energy in biomass is the Sun. Small "factories" in a plant's leaves use light energy from the Sun, together with carbon dioxide from the air and water from the soil, to manufacture sugars, starches and cellulose. The original solar energy is now stored in these chemicals. Some of this energy is passed on to animals when they eat plants. So plants, animals and animal dung – all forms of biomass – are all stores of solar energy. When they burn, they release this chemical energy as light and heat.

◔ Speeding Up Nature

Plant and animal wastes slowly give off heat and the gas methane as they decompose (rot). Worms and insects speed up the rotting process by eating dead material. When we burn biomass we are speeding up this natural process even more.

**Energy
stored as
biomass**

**Rotting
material**

ENERGY FACTS: Not Biofuels!

Coal, gas, oil and other fossil fuels aren't biofuels, even though they were once living plants and animals. They were formed underground over many millions of years, so they can't be considered renewable.

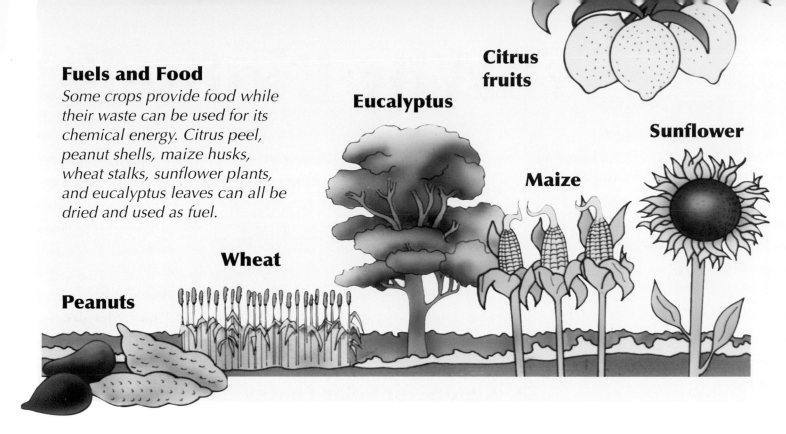

Fuels and Food

Some crops provide food while their waste can be used for its chemical energy. Citrus peel, peanut shells, maize husks, wheat stalks, sunflower plants, and eucalyptus leaves can all be dried and used as fuel.

Citrus fruits

Eucalyptus

Sunflower

Maize

Wheat

Peanuts

Land, Water, Nutrients, Seeds, Energy

Resources are used to grow biomass

Sugar Cane, Maize, Wheat, Rapeseed, Palm Oil, Willow, Switchgrass

Biomass is turned into biofuels

Ethanol, Biodiesel, Biogas, Fuelwood, Charcoal

Biofuels are used to create bioenergy

Transport, heating, electricity

◖ A Renewable Resource

Some forms of biomass, such as trees and crops, are grown specifically to be burnt to generate heat and power. They are a renewable source of energy, but only if enough crops are regrown to replace those that are used as fuel.

The chart on the left shows the links between biomass (energy crops), biofuels (the fuels made from them) and bioenergy (the energy produced by burning these fuels).

◓ Waste

As well as specifically grown crops, biomass includes straw, grain husks, forest products and waste wood.

Why Biofuels?

Biogas and solid fuels such as wood and manure can be used to make the electricity that lights your home, while liquid fuels such as ethanol can be used in cars like fuels made from oil. Organic waste from homes, such as kitchen scraps, can be also burnt to create energy.

Unlike fossil fuels, biofuels are renewable. In theory, they are also carbon neutral. This means that when they are burnt, they release the same amount of carbon dioxide that they take in while growing.

However, some experts argue that using biofuels will not slow global warming. Growing giant fields of energy crops will also take up valuable land needed for growing food and has contributed to rainforest destruction.

Past and Future Fuels

For thousands of years, biofuels were the only fuels used as humans burnt wood for heat and light. Even after the Industrial Revolution, when coal was used to power factories and steam engines, most people used wood for heat and animal fats for light.

In the 20th century, the developed world depended on the energy from oil, gas and coal. Perhaps in the 21st century it will return to using biofuels!

○ **Crops** *have always been an important transport fuel. Two hundred years ago, 20 per cent of farmland in the United States was used to grow fuel for horses and other animals – the original "horse power".*

BIOFUELS: For

• Biofuels are renewable as new crops can be grown every year, but we must plant as many biofuel crops as we use.

• Biofuels tend to be cheap, and will reduce the need to use fossil fuels.

• Unlike some new technology, such as fuel cells, biofuels don't need a new network of filling stations. Biofuels can be mixed with oil-based fuels and used in existing diesel engines.

• Organic waste such as kitchen scraps, sewage and scrap paper can be turned into energy.

▼ Rapeseed Field

Rapeseed is used to create biodiesel for vehicles. It is the world's third largest vegetable oil crop (after soya beans and palm oil).

BIOFUELS: Against

• Collecting or growing the fuel in large enough amounts can be difficult.

• When biofuels are burned, they pollute the air just like fossil fuels. New technology and biofuels based on algae may avoid this.

• Some waste materials are not available all year round.

• If more food crops such as corn or soya beans are used as biofuels, it could push up food prices in the future.

• Energy crops use up valuable farm land.

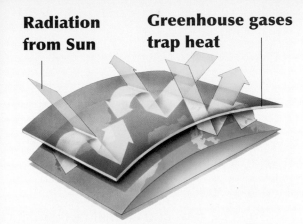

Radiation from Sun

Greenhouse gases trap heat

⚠ What Is Global Warming?

When the Sun's energy reaches the Earth, some is reflected back to space, but most reaches the Earth's surface. Once absorbed, this heat energy is sent back into the atmosphere.

However, "greenhouse" gases such as carbon dioxide and methane trap this heat in the same way that glass traps heat in a greenhouse, causing our world to heat up. Burning fossil fuels such as oil releases large amounts of carbon dioxide, adding to global warming.

Types of Biofuels

People in less developed countries such as Nepal, Ethiopia and Kenya still get most of their energy needs from burning wood, animal dung and other biomass. In more developed countries, most bioenergy still comes from the waste from food and fibre crops such as wheat and wood, despite the growth in biofuels such as ethanol. Forestry waste is turned into wood pellets and charcoal, while farms produce waste straw and cotton stalks.

Animal Dung

In India, sticky cow dung is moulded into tablets then stuck on a wall to dry. It is used as a fuel for cooking, hot water and warmth. Dung from camels, sheep, buffalo and even elephants can be used as fuel.

Energy Crops

Plants grown for their bioenergy are called energy crops, such as sugar cane (pictured below), switchgrass and elephant grass. These all grow tall each year and can be cut down and left to grow for the next harvest.

Waste from Crops

Plants such as wheat and maize are grown for food. However, the stems, or stalks, can be gathered as straw and used as biofuels rather than being wasted.

Harvesting Straw

Industrial Waste

Pulp mills in the US and Canada produce black liquor as waste from processing wood into paper. The energy in the liquor can be used to create steam and generate electricity to power the mills. This avoids polluting fresh water supplies nearby.

❀ Woody Plants

Most commercial forests are grown for timber, but the waste can be made into wood pellets and wood chips. Fast-growing trees such as willow can be cut every two to four years and then harvested by cutting the stems close to the ground. The stumps regrow and can be harvested every few years. Known as coppicing, this method has been used for hundreds of years.

Sugar cane

◐ Peat

Peat is halfway between rotting biomass and coal. It has been used in Europe for hundreds of years in open fires. However, a lot of energy is wasted and it produces high levels of the greenhouse gas carbon dioxide. It is not a renewable energy source, as plants take thousands of years to turn to peat. After millions of years, peat changes into rich black coal.

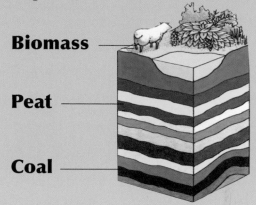

Biomass

Peat

Coal

ENERGY FACTS: Around the World

• Biomass and waste make up around 10 per cent of the world's energy, while fossil fuels make up 80 per cent.
• Asia is the biggest user of biomass that is used for firewood and cooking, followed by Africa. In some countries, up to 90 per cent of energy comes from burning biomass such as fuelwood, charcoal and animal dung.
• India uses 200 million tonnes of fuelwood each year, more than any other country.
• North and South America are the biggest users of liquid biofuels made from energy crops. At present, such fuels account for just 2 per cent of world bioenergy.

Burning Solid Fuels

The simplest way to get energy from biomass is to burn it. But this can be inefficient. An open fireplace allows large amounts of heat to escape, while up to 75 per cent of the energy in solid fuels such as wood simply "goes up in smoke" without burning.

In less developed countries, burning fuelwood is the only way to create heat and light as there is no electricity supply. In more developed countries such as Canada, Finland, Sweden and the United States, solid farm wastes such as wood pellets and straw are burnt in power plants to generate electricity or heat water.

⚠ Fuelwood

This African woman has walked a long way to find fuel for her family.

◑ Charcoal

Charcoal is made by gradually burning wood that smoulders when starved of oxygen. This process, known as pyrolysis, was known to ancient peoples who heaped wood into large piles or buried it before setting fire to it. Charcoal is half the weight of the original wood but contains the same amount of energy. It also burns at a high temperature, making it better for manufacturing. In Brazil, the steel industry uses over two million tonnes of charcoal a year. However, new trees must be grown to replace those cut down.

◑ Charcoal *is a good fuel for barbecues.*

⚠ Wood Stove

Many aid agencies are introducing new stoves to less developed regions. These stoves help fuelwood to last longer. They also produce more heat and give off less harmful fumes.

◆ Straw-fired Power Station

The straw-fired power station at Ely, UK, the largest in the world, can produce 38 megawatts (MW) of electricity, enough to power around 30,000 homes. It uses 200,000 tonnes of straw each year. The straw is burnt in a furnace, fanned by hot air. The heat produced is used to boil water to steam, which is then blasted against turbine blades. As these turn, they drive generators, which produce electricity. To reduce pollution the waste gases are filtered and the ash is recycled as fertiliser.

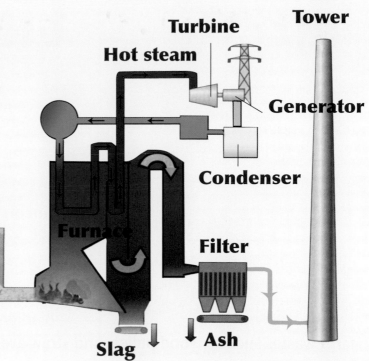

Turbine

Tower

Hot steam

Generator

Condenser

Furnace

Filter

Straw Bales

Conveyor

Slag

Ash

◑ Chicken Power

A power plant in Thetford, Norfolk, UK uses 420,000 tonnes of poultry litter (a mix of chicken droppings and straw) from nearby farms each year. It can provide enough electricity to power around 30,000 homes.

Chicken litter

ENERGY FACTS: Biomass

• When dry biomass reaches a temperature of 200 °C, it gives off gases that mix with oxygen and burn, releasing carbon dioxide.

• A traditional open fire delivers just 16 per cent of the energy contained in wood into a room, while a modern logwood stove delivers about 80 per cent.

◑ Wood-fired Boilers

Wood pellets are made of sawdust and shavings left after cutting trees into timber. At a pellet mill the shavings are dried, compressed and chopped into small pieces.

Wood pellets, wood chips and logs can all be burnt in boilers to heat water. Smaller boilers heat the radiators in a house, while in the town of Siikainen in Finland, larger units are used to heat a whole district.

Wood pellets

Liquid Biofuels

In recent years, more and more biomass has been turned into liquid biofuels. Ethanol, an alcohol, can be made from the sugar in crops such as sugar cane, or from the starch in crops such as maize and wheat. It is produced by fermentation, the same process that creates alcohol in wine and beer. Ethanol is usually mixed with petrol. In Sweden E-85 (85 per cent ethanol) fuel is partly made from the waste from wine-making in southern Europe.

Biodiesel is made from plants that contain high amounts of vegetable oil. It can be used neat or mixed with normal diesel. B-20 (20 per cent biodiesel) is a popular fuel in trucks because it helps to lubricate the engine.

▶ Turning Sugar into Fuel

For centuries, people have used yeasts to ferment the sugar of various plants into ethanol.

Producing fuel from biomass by fermentation can be done with many different crops, including sweet sorghum, sugar beet, sugar cane, wheat, maize and cassava.

Running on Vegetable Oil

German inventor Rudolph Diesel designed his engines to run on biofuels. Biodiesel is produced by combining vegetable oils with alcohol. In Europe and the United States, the oil is taken from oily crops such as rapeseed and soya beans. Coconut oil is used in tractors in the Philippines, while sunflower oil is used in South Africa. Biodiesel can also be made from animal fats or recycled cooking oil.

Biofuel Buses

Since 1975, Brazil has been a leading developer of biofuels, mainly using ethanol produced from sugar cane. The programme has been a great success, and today most buses in Brazil run on pure ethanol (E-100) or a mix of ethanol and petrol, known as gasohol. Sixty per cent of new cars in Brazil can also run on a fuel mix which includes 85 per cent ethanol.

Harvesting sugar cane

Ethanol car – *the* Obvio! *can run on pure ethanol (E-100).*

13

Biogas

Natural gas, a fossil fuel found underground, is mainly methane. Methane forms when plants rot in places where there is no air. Landfill gas is methane that builds up underground as rubbish is broken down by bacteria. This biogas can be collected. After it is mixed with carbon dioxide, it can be burned like natural gas for cooking or heating, or used to generate electricity.

Biogas can also be produced from animal or human waste in a digester. However, because of its low methane content, this biogas can't be used to fuel vehicles unless it is treated and compressed like Liquified Natural Gas (LNG).

Digestion

Digestion is a way of using bacteria to create biogas. These tiny organisms usually live at the bottom of swamps where there is no air. When they consume dead organic matter, they produce methane and hydrogen. We can put these bacteria to work by adding them to tanks of human or animal waste, called digesters. Up to two-thirds of the energy of the animal dung is turned into fuel and the remains are used as fertiliser.

A digester *being built from bricks.*

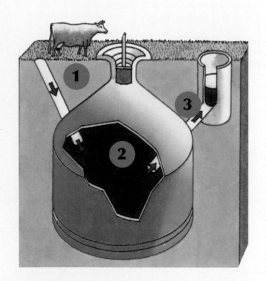

How a digester works

1 *Animal dung or human sewage is fed into tanks called digesters.*
2 *Bacteria are added to the fermentation chamber.*
3 *The bacteria produce methane, which is tapped and collected, then piped to homes.*

Biogas gasifier

◐ Gasification

We can also turn solid fuels such as wood into biogas using a process known as gasification. Gasifiers burn biomass at high temperatures, starving it of oxygen. The solid fuels give off an energy-rich synthetic gas, or syngas.

Syngas can be burned in a boiler to heat a home, used like natural gas for cooking, or in a gas turbine to turn electric generators. Gasification also removes harmful chemicals, so when syngas is burnt it produces less pollution than the wood it came from.

◐ Landfill Sites

We can collect gas from landfill sites. Biomass waste, such as kitchen scraps, ends up at the local tip. Over several decades, bacteria steadily decompose this organic matter, giving off the gas methane. This can be extracted by "capping" a landfill site with a layer of clay. Pipes collect the gas and bring it to the surface, where it is processed and piped to homes, or used to generate electricity.

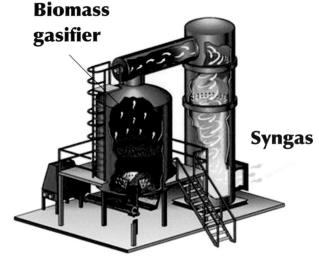

Biomass gasifier

Syngas

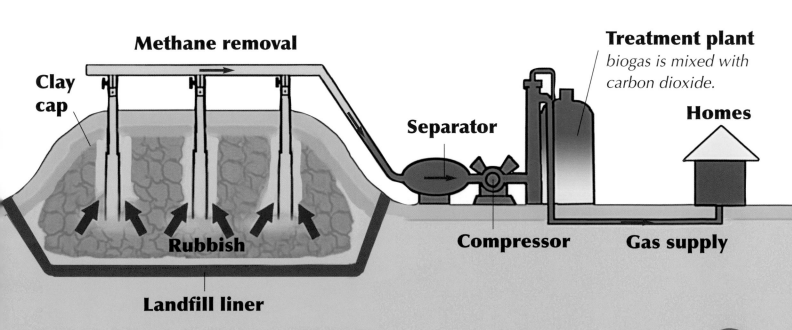

Methane removal

Clay cap

Rubbish

Landfill liner

Separator

Compressor

Treatment plant
biogas is mixed with carbon dioxide.

Homes

Gas supply

Electricity from Waste

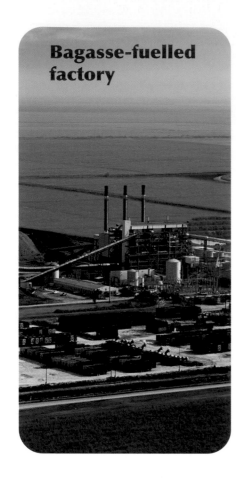

Bagasse-fuelled factory

Some power plants burn rubbish and sewage. The heat turns water into steam, which is used to heat buildings or generate electricity. Some are Combined Heat and Power plants that capture hot exhaust gases and use them to heat nearby homes.

Burning waste also cuts down on the amount of waste in landfills. In the United States, 90 waste-to-energy plants dispose of the waste of 40 million people and generate electricity for three million homes. However, they release greenhouse gases and harmful chemicals into the air.

From Pulp to Power

When the juice has been removed from cut sugar cane to make sugar, the leftover pulp remains. Known as bagasse, this waste makes good fuel. At the Florida Crystals sugar mill, 850,000 tonnes of bagasse is burnt each year to power the factory (left). Along with other biomass, it also creates electricity for 60,000 local homes in Palm Beach County, Florida.

Danger from Pollution

Burning waste reduces the need for ugly landfills (pictured below). The waste is burned at very high temperatures (1000 ºC) to produce heat. Though this breaks down some dangerous chemicals, others, such as mercury and chlorine, are still released into the air. Another challenge is getting rid of the ash, which also contains high levels of harmful chemicals.

ENERGY FACTS:
Biomass Power

• For each 100 tonnes of sugar cane it crushes, a sugar factory produces 30 tonnes of wet bagasse.

• 1 hectare of sugar cane can yield 7,500 litres of ethanol, enough to power 60 to 90 homes for a year.

• CHP (combined heat and power) generators are twice as efficient (80 per cent) as power plants that burn biomass only to generate electricity.

• Rubbish does not contain as much heat energy as coal. It takes four tonnes of garbage to equal the heat energy in 1 tonne of coal.

CHP plant

⬣ Combined Heat and Power (CHP)

Conventional power plants that burn coal or biomass to make electricity release the heat into the air. Combined heat and power plants capture this heat and use it to produce more electricity or to heat the local district.

It's an old idea – Thomas Edison's Pearl Street Station (1882), the world's first power plant, produced electricity and used the waste heat to warm neighbouring buildings.

◁ Local CHP Plant

Houses in Hammarby Sjöstad, a suburb in Stockholm, Sweden, are heated by a system first used in the 1960s. Household rubbish is sucked along pipes to a separator. Metals and glass are removed and sent to be recycled while suitable rubbish is burned in a CHP plant. This provides electricity and heat via a district heating system.

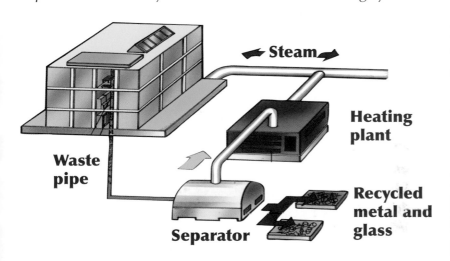

Steam

Heating plant

Waste pipe

Separator

Recycled metal and glass

▷ Micro CHP

CHP units the size of a normal boiler can be fitted into homes and factories. Instead of burning fuel to merely heat space or water, some of the energy is converted to electricity which can be sold back into the power grid.

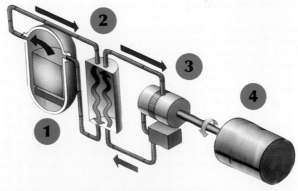

Generating Electricity

1 *The biomass is burnt in a furnace.*

2 *The heat boils water into steam.*

3 *The steam turns the blades of a turbine.*

4 *The turbine is connected by a shaft to a generator. Inside the generator, the shaft makes magnets spin inside wire coils, which produces electricity.*

Biomass and Fuel Cells

When biomass such as wood is gasified, it gives off hydrogen along with other gases such as carbon monoxide. Hydrogen is not an energy source, but it can be used in fuel cells to power cars. Unlike batteries, fuel cells don't store electrical energy. Instead, they convert energy from chemical reactions between oxygen and hydrogen directly into electrical energy. Fuel cells can generate enough power to supply cars, office blocks, hospitals, submarines and spacecraft.

⬟ Powered by Hydrogen

Hydrogen could power cars of the future via fuel cells. Several test cars have already been built by different manufacturers. In 2004, a fuel cell car (above) drove across Europe. Fuel cells are very quiet and produce no exhaust fumes. However, hydrogen is expensive to produce and difficult to handle. Today's fuel cells are often heavy and expensive, but they will get smaller and cheaper.

⬟ Silent Running

The German submarine U 212A is powered by fuel cells. These allow it to stay submerged for up to three weeks without surfacing and with no exhaust heat. The engine is also extremely quiet and virtually undetectable.

► How a Fuel Cell Works

Scientist William Grove produced the first fuel cell over 150 years ago. He knew that sending an electric current through water splits the water into hydrogen and oxygen. Grove tried reversing the reaction, combining hydrogen and oxygen to produce electricity and water. This is how a simple fuel cell works. The hydrogen from gasified biomass can be used directly in fuel cells to power electric cars and other vehicles.

1 *Hydrogen (H) and oxygen (O₂) flow into fuel cell.*

2 *Hydrogen combines with oxygen.*

3 *Electricity is created as the gases form water (H₂O).*

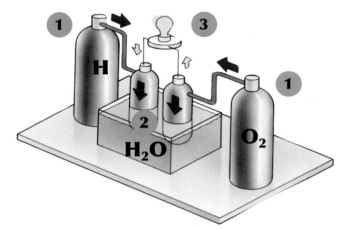

Fuel cell

Hydrogen from Wood Chips

Tomorrow's fuel-cell vehicles may be powered by special proteins that consume cellulose from woodchips or grass and release hydrogen. These proteins, known as enzymes, are produced in plants to start and speed up chemical reactions. Crop waste and switchgrass could also be used to create sugar-to-hydrogen fuel cells for cars and trucks.

► Out in Space

Fuel cells have no major moving parts, so they are also very reliable, one reason why they are used to power space shuttles far out in space. Also, unlike a battery, a fuel cell doesn't run down or need recharging. It continues to produce electricity as long as fuel (hydrogen) is supplied.

Space shuttle

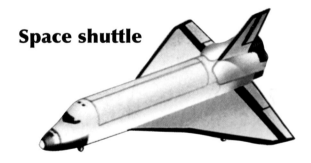

Inside a Fuel Cell Car

1 *Tanks store hydrogen*
2 *Air pump (draws in oxygen to mix with hydrogen in fuel cell)*
3 *Fuel cells create electricity*
4 *Battery stores electricity*
5 *Electric engine*
6 *Power Drive Unit controls flow of electricity*

Can Biofuels Work?

Biofuels currently supply just 2 per cent of fuels used by transport, but one day they could supply some 30 per cent of global demand. Today, most liquid biofuels are produced from food crops such as corn because processing this into ethanol is fairly easy. However, a lot of energy is wasted, and using food crops for energy forced up food prices during 2007-2008.

Most experts agree that biofuels made from energy crops cannot solve global warming or replace fossil fuels on their own. But they could work as part of bigger schemes combining renewables such as wind and solar power with new ways of using energy more efficiently.

◆ Renewable Energy

One of the big advantages of biomass is that it is renewable – plants can be harvested and grown again the following year. Fast-growing mallee trees (above) are being planted in Western Australia and can be harvested every few years.

◆ A Good Use of Farmland?

Energy crops are not an efficient use of farmland. To replace oil, it would take some 4 million square km of land to produce enough ethanol to fuel vehicles in the United States – more than all the available farmland.

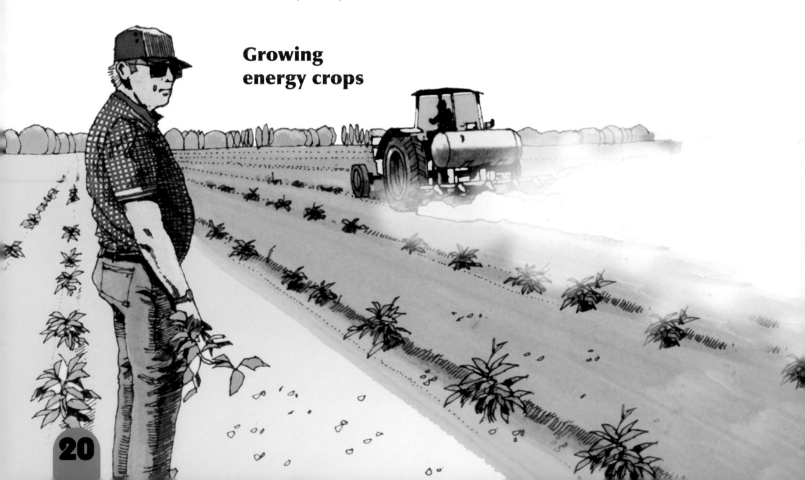

Growing energy crops

Wheat harvest

⬤ A Threat to Food?

If more farmers grow energy crops for biofuels instead of food, it could cause food prices to rise. However, this will be avoided if farm wastes such as straw are used, rather than the parts of the crop that are eaten. Some 75 per cent of the world's poor still make a living from farming, and biofuels could provide them with an income and a cheap source of energy.

⬤ Easy to Use

Petrol and diesel engines can easily be adapted to run on biofuels. This gives biofuels an advantage over other forms of renewable energy, such as wind or solar power, which can power only electric vehicles. Meanwhile, biogas from landfill and sewage can be used just like natural gas to heat homes or for cooking.

Biofuel pump in Brazil

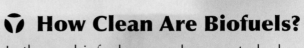

⬤ How Clean Are Biofuels?

In theory, biofuels are carbon-neutral – burning a plant releases no more carbon than it took in while it was growing. Ethanol and biodiesel also release less pollution into the air than petrol and diesel.

However, when trees are burned to make way for energy crops, huge amounts of carbon dioxide are released. It would take hundreds of years for soya or maize to take in the same amount of carbon.

⬤ Habitat Destruction

One fear is that a big switch to biofuels will reduce the natural habitats of wild animals and plants even further.

Indonesia has burned so much wilderness to grow palm oil trees for biodiesel that it is now the world's third highest producer of the greenhouse gas carbon dioxide.

The Future of Biofuels

🜂 Jatropha

Scientists are looking into new energy crops, such as jatropha. The railway line between Mumbai and Delhi is planted with jatropha and the train itself runs on biodiesel.

Biofuels are already an important source of energy in many countries. Over the next 100 years, they may also replace fossil fuels on a large scale. Local forms of biomass, such as straw, seaweed, or wood, may work better than giant fields of energy crops. Using biomass from farm and human waste will avoid using precious farmland needed for growing food crops.

New biofuels are being developed from the cellulose in the parts of crops that we don't eat, such as the stalks. This would allow us to produce ethanol from a much greater range of plants. Research is also being done into fast-growing seaweeds to see if they can be used to produce biofuels.

Jet Biofuels

In 2008, Virgin Atlantic became the first airline to fly a jumbo jet (from London to Sydney) using a mix of 75 per cent normal jet fuel and 25 per cent biofuels. These came from a mix of coconut and babassu oil.

In the same year, the US firm Solazyme produced the world's first jet biofuel made from algae. The company grows algae in tanks shielded from the Sun, feeding the algae sugars rather than light.

Jumbo jet

Keep It Local

Transporting bulky biomass such as wood and plant waste uses up energy, so to remain carbon neutral, biomass power plants should be close to their source of fuel. Every city could convert its human and organic waste and biomass into fuel in local plants.

▷ Marifuels

Scientists in Scotland and Japan are looking at ways to convert sea plants, particularly kelp, a fast-growing species, into fuel. Large nets could be placed off the coast to harvest other plants such as sea grape. The fuel could provide remote communities with a cheap, local source of fuel.

Kelp

◁ Seaweed Farms

In the future, seaweed could be grown on large offshore farms. This could produce fuel without using good farmland used for food crops.

GM (Genetically Modified) Energy Crops

Genetically improving fast-growing energy crops such as switchgrass and poplar may speed up the growing process. Swiss biotech firm Syngenta is developing a GM maize that is easy to convert into ethanol thanks to a special enzyme.

Other scientists are designing trees that have less lignin, the strength-giving substance that enables them to stand upright, but makes it more difficult to convert the tree's cellulose into ethanol. However, environmentalists are worried that these altered trees will cross-breed with wild trees.

◁ GM scientists at work

Fuel from Algae

One of the most exciting developments in recent years is biofuels made from algae – what you might recognise as green pond scum. Scientists hope to develop the new fuel so that any regular car can fill its tank with it at a local petrol station.

While some scientific teams are trying to breed more oily algae, others are finding cheaper ways to harvest the algae or refine the oil. The final challenge is finding a way to mass-produce the fuel cheaply and encourage motorists around the world to make the switch from petrol or diesel.

Bioreactors *allow large amounts of algae to be grown in a small area.*

What Are Algae?

Algae can be found almost everywhere – from seas and ponds to fish tanks. Like plants, these single-celled organisms can turn sunshine into chemical energy. Some species even create oils similar to the vegetable oil that is used to produce biodiesel. The big difference is that algae are incredibly efficient at turning light, water and carbon dioxide into chemical energy – around 20 to 200 times higher than crops like soya beans.

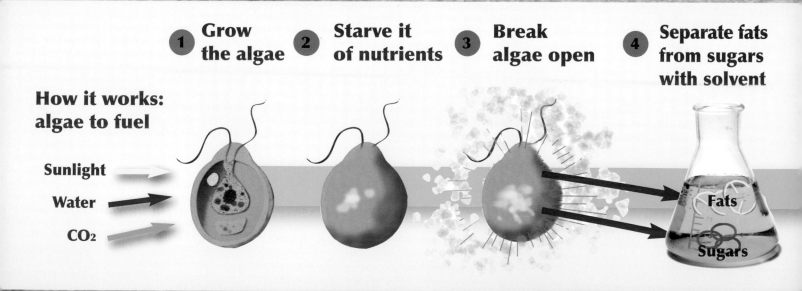

1 Grow the algae **2** Starve it of nutrients **3** Break algae open **4** Separate fats from sugars with solvent

How it works: algae to fuel

Sunlight

Water

CO_2

Fats

Sugars

▷ Algae Farms

Algae can grow incredibly quickly in the right conditions. To farm algae on a large scale, however, the water needs to be just the right temperature. Extra carbon dioxide needs to be pumped in to promote fast growth. There is also a danger of other plants invading.

To solve these problems, some firms are planning to farm algae in bioreactors – bags or tubes made from plastic sheets. Water and carbon dioxide can then be pumped in while the enclosed algae are cut off from invading plants.

No Waste

Algae is harvested by using chemicals to make it clump together or bubbles to make it froth to the surface. After the algae is refined and the oil extracted, nothing is wasted. The water is recycled and since it is trapped in bioreactors, very little evaporates into the air. The biomass that remains after the oil is taken out can also be used to make animal feed.

Carbon Capture

One of the biggest advantages of using algae to make biofuels is that you don't need farmland to grow it – the bioreactors or ponds sit on top of the ground. Also, algae gobble up carbon dioxide (a greenhouse gas) and nitrogen dioxide (a pollutant). Building algae farms close to power plants and factories that give off these gases would reduce air pollution and slow global warming. Algae can eat just about anything in order to make oil. In the future, some algae farms may convert plant or animal waste into energy.

5 **Evaporate solvent** **6** **Turn fats into biodiesel** **7** **Biodiesel**

Fats

HOT OFF THE PRESS

Cow's about that!

■ A German town will become the first in the world to be powered by animal waste when it launches a biogas network this year.

Lünen, north of Dortmund, will use cow and horse manure as well as other crop waste from local farms to provide 30-40 per cent of the town's heat and electricity needs.

The biomass will be fed into heated tanks, where bacteria will break it down into methane and carbon dioxide. This biogas can then be burned to generate electricity and heat in a

Cow manure naturally gives off the biogas methane.

combined heat and power plant (CHP). The heat will then be distributed across the town through an underground pipeline. Despite the use of manure as fuel, residents shouldn't expect to have nasty smells flooding their living rooms every time they turn the heating on.

Biogas powers college

■ The University of New Hampshire is the first in the United States to run on methane gas from a nearby landfill. The university will get 85 per cent of its heat and electricity from the project, known as Ecofill, which should take around 10 years to pay back its building costs. Any extra electricity produced will be fed back in to the electric power grid.

Sweet speedster

■ Scientists from the University of Warwick in England have designed a Formula 3 racing car that runs on vegetable oils and chocolate waste that has been turned into biofuel.

The steering wheel is made out of fibres derived from carrots and other root vegetables, and the bodywork is made of plant fibres from potatoes.

The team hope the car will reach speeds of 230 km/h when it is driven at full speed around a racetrack.

The chocolate racer

Turning chocolate into hydrogen

■ Researchers from the University of Birmingham, UK, have found a way to produce hydrogen by feeding caramel and nougat waste from a chocolate factory to *E. coli* bacteria.

The bacteria fermented the sugars in the chocolate waste. This created organic acids so poisonous to the bacteria that they began converting the acids to hydrogen like mad. The researchers then used the hydrogen to power a fuel cell, which generated enough electricity to run a small fan. The discovery of a way to extract hydrogen from food waste could be a real breakthrough, especially if it works just as well on other types of waste. So next time you munch into a bar of chocolate, you could be helping to save the planet!

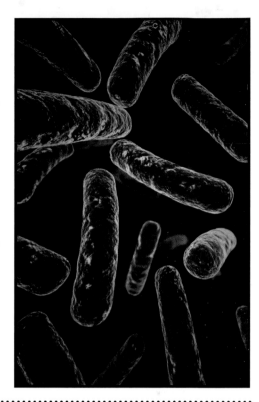

E. coli bacteria can be used to manufacture hydrogen, a very clean fuel.

Poop power

■ San Francisco is the first city in the United States to consider turning pet poop into methane that can be used for fuel. American dogs and cats produce 10 million tonnes of waste a year, and a lot of it goes into landfills. In San Francisco, for example, pet poop accounts for nearly 4 per cent of the city's waste.

The city plans to place

" American dogs and cats produce 10 million tonnes of waste a year, and a lot of it goes into landfills. **"**

dog-waste carts in one of the city's busiest dog parks, collect the waste and toss it into a digester. This will use bacteria to convert animal waste to methane in about two weeks.

Charcoal solution

■ Charcoal, also known as biochar, may be able to make a dent on global warming. Some experts argue that farm waste should be turned into charcoal and then buried or sunk in the ocean. This would trap the greenhouse gases given off if the waste was left to rot.

Farmers can turn their waste into carbon using a charcoal maker. Some of the charcoal could be sold as fuel or fertilizer, so the whole process could pay for itself.

Biochar can also be mixed with compost to fertilise the soil.

How Biofuels Compare

While fossil fuels are cheap, they release carbon dioxide into the atmosphere, causing pollution and global warming. Nuclear power can create a lot of energy, but reactors are expensive and create dangerous waste. Though biofuels and other renewables such as wind power are cleaner sources of energy, they supply just a small part of the world's energy needs.

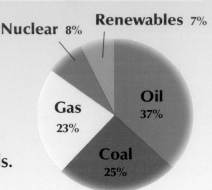

World Energy Sources

Nuclear 8% Renewables 7%
Oil 37%
Gas 23%
Coal 25%

NON-RENEWABLE ENERGY SOURCES

Oil

For:

Oil is cheap and easy to store, transport and use.

Against:

Oil is not renewable and it is getting more expensive to get out of the ground. Burning oil releases large amounts of greenhouse gases. Oil spills, especially at sea, cause severe pollution.

Gas

For:

Gas is relatively cheap, and produces less greenhouses gases than oil and coal.

Against:

Burning gas releases carbon dioxide. Gas is not renewable and the world's natural gas reserves are limited. Gas pipelines can disrupt the migration routes of animals such as caribou.

Coal

For:

Coal is cheap and supplies of coal are expected to last another 150 years.

Against:

Coal-fired power stations give off the most greenhouse gases. They also produce sulphur dioxide, creating acid rain. Coal mining can be very destructive to the landscape.

Nuclear

For:

Nuclear power is constant and reliable, and doesn't contribute to global warming.

Against:

Not renewable as uranium (the main nuclear fuel) will eventually run out. Nuclear waste is so dangerous it must be buried for thousands of years. Also the risk of a nuclear accident.

RENEWABLE ENERGY SOURCES

Biofuels

For:

Biofuels are cheap and renewable and can be made from waste.

Against:

Growing biofuels from energy crops reduces the land available for food and uses up vital resources such as fresh water. Like fossil fuels, biofuels can produce greenhouse gases.

Wind Power

For:

Wind power needs no fuel, it's renewable and doesn't pollute.

Against:

Wind is unpredictable, so wind farms need a back-up power supply. Possible danger to bird flocks. It takes thousands of wind turbines to produce the same power as a nuclear plant.

Solar Power

For:

Solar power needs no fuel, it's renewable and doesn't pollute.

Against:

Solar power stations are very expensive as solar (photovoltaic) cells cost a lot compared to the amount of electricity they produce. They're unreliable unless used in a very sunny climate.

Hydroelectric Power

For:

Hydroelectric power needs no fuel, is renewable and doesn't pollute.

Against:

Hydroelectric is very expensive to build. A big dam will flood a very large area upstream, impacting on animals and people there. A dam can also affect water quality downstream.

Geothermal Power

For:

Geothermal power needs no fuel, it's renewable and doesn't pollute.

Against:

There aren't many suitable places for a geothermal power station as you need hot rocks of the right type and not too deep. It can "run out of steam". Underground poisonous gases can be a danger.

Tidal Power

For:

Tidal power needs no fuel, is reliable, renewable and doesn't pollute.

Against:

Tidal power machines are expensive to build and only provide power for around 10 hours each day, when the tide is actually moving in or out. Not an efficient way of producing electricity.

Glossary and Resources

algae Organisms that live in water and store the Sun's light as chemicals, ranging in size from a single cell to a giant kelp.

atmosphere The thick blanket of air that surrounds the Earth.

bacteria A major group of tiny organisms shaped like spheres, rods or spirals.

bagasse The pulp left behind after the juice has been removed from sugar cane.

biodiesel Biofuel made from oils in plants such as rapeseed and soya beans.

biofuel A fuel produced from biomass.

biogas Gas produced from biomass, especially methane.

biomass Plant and animal matter used to make biofuels.

chemical energy The energy stored in organic matter such as plants.

CHP Combined Heat and Power, describing a power station that produces electricity and heat for a local district.

decompose To rot.

digester A tank in which biomass rots and gives off biogas.

ethanol A form of alcohol that can be used as a biofuel.

ferment To break down a substance using yeast or bacteria.

fossil fuel A fuel such as coal, oil or gas that is formed underground from the remains of prehistoric plants and animals.

fuel cell A device that combines hydrogen and oxygen to create electricity that can be used to power an electric car.

gasification Converting solids or liquids into gas.

generator A machine that turns mechanical energy into electrical energy.

global warming A warming of the Earth's surface. Many scientists predict that global warming may lead to more floods, droughts and rising sea levels.

GM Plants or animals that have been changed by genetic engineering.

greenhouse effect The global warming caused by human-made gases, such as carbon dioxide and methane, that trap the heat from the Sun in the atmosphere.

megawatt (MW) A million watts (a watt is a unit of power), or 1,000 kilowatts (kW).

power station A plant where electricity is generated.

renewable Something that can be used over and over without running out.

sewage Human waste.

turbine A machine with rotating blades that turn a shaft, usually connected to a generator.

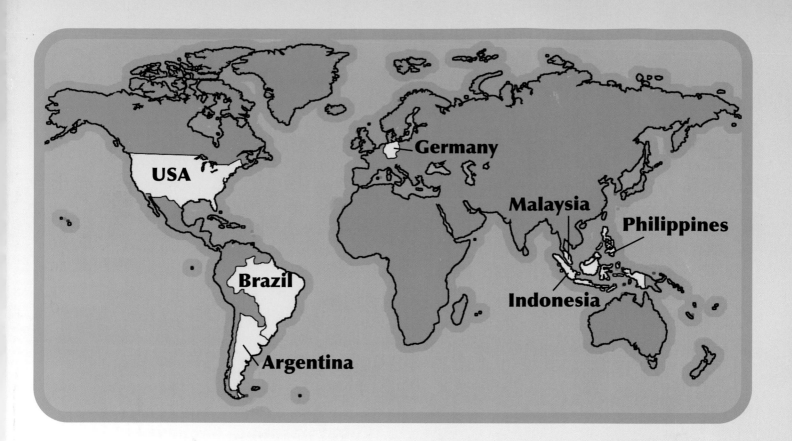

Useful Websites

If you're interested in finding out more about biofuels, the following websites are helpful:

www.therenewableenergycentre.co.uk
www.alternative-energy-
   news.info/technology/biofuels/
www.eia.doe.gov/kids/energyfacts/
   sources/renewable/biomass.html
www.biofuels4schools.org/
www.bioenergycenter.org/students-
   and-kids/

ENERGY FACTS: Biofuels World Map

These countries are likely to become the top biofuel producers in the future:

- **USA** – maize (ethanol) and soya beans (biodiesel)
- **Brazil** – sugar cane (ethanol), soya beans and sunflower seeds (biodiesel)
- **Malaysia** – palm oil (biodiesel)
- **Indonesia** – palm oil (biodiesel)
- **Argentina** – soya beans (biodiesel) and sugar cane (ethanol)
- **Philippines** – sugar cane (ethanol), coconut oil and jatropha (biodiesel)
- **Germany** – rapeseed (biodiesel), cereals and sugar beet (ethanol)

Further Reading

World Issues: Energy Crisis by Ewan McLeish (Aladdin/Watts)
Issues in Our World: Energy Crisis by Ewan McLeish (Aladdin/Watts)
Your Environment: Future Energy by Sally Morgan (Aladdin/Watts)
Saving Our World: New Energy Sources by Nigel Hawkes (Aladdin/Watts)
Our World: Future Energy by Jen Green (Aladdin/Watts)
Energy Sources: Biomass Power by Neil Morris (Franklin Watts)

Index

Photocredits

(Abbreviations: t – top, m – middle, b – bottom, l – left, r – right).

All photos istockphoto.com except: 3tl, 18b: Siemens press picture. 5br, 18br: courtesy Shell. 9ml: John Deere. 13mr: courtesy Obvio! 16ml: courtesy Florida Crystals Corporation. 18tr: courtesy BP. 19br: courtesy Honda. 20tr: Surabky/www.dreamstime.com. 22tr: courtesy Thernergo. 22br: Virgin Airlines. 23bl: courtesy Syngenta. 24ml: Valcent Products Inc. 25tr: courtesy A2BE Carbon Capture, LLC. 26b: courtesy Warwick Innovative Manufacturing Research Centre, UK.